Copilot in Microsoft Teams

AI for Smarter Collaboration

Dr. Patrick Jones

OLYMPUS ACADEMY
PRESS

The Microsoft Teams Companion Series

The Microsoft Teams Companion Series

Welcome to *The Microsoft Teams Companion Series*—your step-by-step guide to mastering every aspect of Microsoft Teams. Each book in this collection covers a distinct area, ensuring that by the end, you'll possess an in-depth, holistic understanding of Teams for personal use, business, education, or enterprise-level deployments.

Here's what you'll find in this series:

1. *Introduction to Microsoft Teams*

2. *Teams & Channels*

3. *Chats & Meetings*

4. *Teams Phones*

5. *Apps & Integrations*

6. *Copilot in Microsoft Teams*

7. *Accessibility in Microsoft Teams*

8. *Microsoft Teams in Education*

9. *Security, Compliance, and Administration in Microsoft Teams*

10. *Expert Tips & Troubleshooting: Becoming a Microsoft Teams Power User*

Looking to dive even deeper into the Microsoft ecosystem? Explore our other companion series—*The Microsoft 365 Companion Series, The Microsoft Intune Companion Series, and The Microsoft Purview Companion Series*—all available on Amazon. Each provides the same clear, comprehensive coverage you'll find here, helping you expand and refine your skills across the full spectrum of Microsoft products and services.

TABLE OF CONTENTS

CHAPTER 1: INTRODUCING COPILOT IN MICROSOFT TEAMS

Most of us have heard about AI assistants in one form or another—smartphone helpers that answer questions, scheduling tools that suggest meeting times, or chatbots that guide you through a website. But Copilot in Microsoft Teams is different. It doesn't merely respond to a quick question or handle a single task; it lives right alongside your regular Teams features, supporting your everyday work with context-aware suggestions, automated summaries, and more. In this opening chapter, we'll define what Copilot actually is, explain why AI-driven features are poised to transform workplace communication, and outline what you can expect to learn in the rest of this book. Finally, we'll peek in on Sarah from 365 Strategies, who just heard about Copilot's pilot program and wonders how this AI might lighten her daily workload and reduce busywork.

Before diving into details, let's get a clear sense of where Copilot fits in. Microsoft 365 is the larger ecosystem that includes Word, Excel, PowerPoint, Outlook, and of course, Microsoft Teams. Over the past few years, Microsoft has introduced more and more intelligent features—like improved grammar suggestions, data analysis helpers in Excel, or quick design ideas in PowerPoint. Copilot can be seen as the next step in that evolution: a more advanced AI-driven assistant that's woven into different parts of Microsoft 365, with Teams as a central focus.

Think of Copilot as a digital collaborator who not only knows how to handle tasks within Teams—like summarizing a conversation or helping schedule a meeting—but also understands context from across

Microsoft 365. If you're discussing a project file in a Teams channel, Copilot might suggest relevant content from SharePoint or pull key data from Excel. Its ability to "see" information from various Microsoft services (where your permissions allow) makes it more powerful than assistants that exist only in a single app.

Because of this cross-service awareness, Copilot can help with tasks that span multiple apps—like drafting an email summary of a Teams conversation, referencing attachments from OneDrive, or aligning your Outlook calendar schedules with meeting notes in OneNote. Over time, you can expect Copilot to gain more advanced capabilities, but even the early features have the potential to reshape how you and your coworkers interact within Teams.

You might ask, "How is Copilot any different from the voice assistant on my phone, or from a chatbot that answers basic questions?" The answer lies in its direct integration with your corporate data and collaboration tools. Personal voice assistants usually cater to individual tasks—like setting a timer or playing music. Chatbots on websites often only handle simple FAQs. Copilot, on the other hand, is designed to:

- Work within your organization's environment: It respects your company's security, data, and permissions, so it doesn't reveal sensitive information to unauthorized people.

- Handle multi-step tasks: Rather than just responding to one command, it can gather information from a Teams channel, suggest follow-up actions, create quick summaries, or even propose next steps for a project.

- Provide context-aware suggestions: If you're in a chat discussing upcoming deadlines, Copilot might proactively offer to schedule a meeting or present a short recap of what's been decided so far.

In short, Copilot is less about general knowledge queries and more about assisting with real, day-to-day collaboration within Microsoft 365—particularly inside Teams. That distinction is important because it means the AI's main purpose isn't to be a know-it-all search engine, but a contextual helper that speeds up your work routines.

We live in an era where daily job requirements are increasingly digital. We manage projects, chat with colleagues, share documents, schedule meetings—all online. While the technology is convenient, it can also be overwhelming. Email inboxes overflow, chats pile up, and files scatter across multiple SharePoint sites. Even scheduling a single meeting can involve a long thread of back-and-forth messages.

AI-driven features address these challenges by handling the repetitive, time-consuming parts of your workflow. Instead of manually combing through a long chat thread to see who promised to do what, an AI might highlight the main action items. Instead of searching multiple calendars for a possible meeting slot, the AI can propose one that fits everyone's typical availability. Instead of re-checking multiple documents to find where a specific agreement was made, the AI might locate it with a simple command. The idea is that by letting the AI do the "grunt work," you and your coworkers can focus on the human aspects—like decision-making, creativity, or building relationships.

Among the most frequent complaints in modern workplaces is information overload: we get messages in multiple chats, threads, and emails, making it tough to recall who said what or which tasks have been assigned. Copilot can drastically reduce that load by automatically generating *summaries of chat discussions* or *pinpointing key points in a conversation*. For scheduling, it can help you find a meeting time faster by scanning participants' Outlook calendars. For task management, it might soon highlight pending deadlines or unassigned items.

Another pain point is context switching—jumping between different apps or windows to accomplish one project. With Copilot's cross-app awareness, you might spend less time toggling between Word, Excel, Teams, and Outlook. If you're discussing a spreadsheet in Teams, for instance, Copilot can bring relevant data from Excel or OneDrive straight into the chat, making the conversation more productive and anchored in real data. The overarching vision is to minimize your daily overhead tasks, so you can channel that energy into more meaningful, creative work.

As you progress through this book, you'll learn about Copilot's different capabilities, the technical underpinnings that let it navigate your Microsoft 365 environment, and best practices for using it effectively in a team setting. We'll cover topics like:

- Setting up Copilot: Understanding licensing requirements, initial configuration steps, and how IT might enable or limit certain features.

- Core features: Summaries of chats, meeting transcripts, advanced scheduling suggestions, and how Copilot can act on your behalf if you want it to.

- Use cases: Automating routine tasks, analyzing conversation sentiment, generating action items, and integrating with other data within Microsoft 365.

- Governance and security: How to ensure your company's data remains protected, dealing with compliance concerns, and clarifying the boundaries of what Copilot can and cannot access.

By the end of the book, you should feel comfortable understanding what Copilot does, deciding when it can be most helpful, and shaping your team's workflows to leverage AI's strengths. We'll keep the explanations straightforward—no heavy technical jargon or advanced coding knowledge required. If you simply want to harness AI to reduce busywork, you're in the right place.

Sarah Hears About Copilot's Pilot Program at 365 Strategies

At 365 Strategies, Sarah's been juggling multiple Teams channels—her department's chat, cross-functional project channels, and direct messages about upcoming campaigns. She often feels like she's losing track of the final decisions or next steps buried in the threads. One day, she overhears her manager discussing a "Copilot pilot program." The manager casually says, "We might get an AI assistant inside Teams to help with scheduling and summarizing chats. Could be a game-changer for us."

Curious, Sarah logs into Teams and sees a new info post from IT about a limited Copilot rollout. It mentions features like automatic conversation summaries and advanced scheduling. She wonders if this is the solution to her daily email chaos and missed chat updates. She's also slightly skeptical—will an AI tool actually get it right, or just add more confusion?

Still, she's intrigued. If Copilot can cut down the time she spends searching for who agreed to handle which deliverable, it might free her up to focus on planning marketing campaigns. She signs up to be part of the pilot group, hoping that by testing Copilot early, she can shape its development and show her team the benefits. As she closes her laptop for the day, Sarah imagines a near future where her daily stand-up tasks are automatically summarized, and routine scheduling becomes a single-click affair.

Copilot represents a new chapter in how AI weaves itself into everyday teamwork—far beyond simple chatbots or personal voice assistants. Its ability to bridge information and tasks from multiple Microsoft 365 services, all from within Teams, offers a way to tackle some of the biggest headaches in modern collaboration, like finding relevant documents or recapping lengthy discussions. As we move forward, we'll explore Copilot's core functionalities, how it integrates with your existing environment, best practices for adoption, and the potential road ahead for AI in the workplace.

Sarah's story highlights the promise of Copilot: an AI that not only automates repetitive chores but also brings clarity and context to your workflows. In the next chapters, we'll dive deeper into how it's set up, what it can and cannot do, and how to ensure it respects your organization's data and compliance requirements. Strap in—AI-driven collaboration is poised to reshape how we communicate, and Copilot could be the extra pair of hands (or eyes) you never knew you needed.

CHAPTER 2: THE AI UNDERPINNINGS OF COPILOT

Copilot in Microsoft Teams might feel like magic—summarizing chats, suggesting meeting times, or highlighting important documents—all in the flow of your daily work. But behind this user-friendly experience lies a deep technology stack that handles natural language processing (NLP), sifts through relevant data in your Microsoft 365 environment, and respects security boundaries to ensure that only authorized content is revealed. This chapter aims to unpack how Copilot's underlying AI models function, how data and permissions flow through the system, and what ethical guidelines govern this advanced technology. Finally, we'll check in with Sarah at 365 Strategies, who's learning the ins and outs of Copilot's data handling from her IT team.

At its core, Copilot leverages what's called a Large Language Model (LLM)—a specialized AI engine that's been trained on massive amounts of text. This training helps the model understand and generate natural-sounding language. LLMs can figure out context, infer intentions, and respond with relevant summaries or recommendations. For instance, if you ask Copilot to "Summarize the discussion from yesterday's marketing channel," it won't merely provide random sentences; it processes the entire conversation, extracting key points and creating a concise overview.

Unlike basic chatbots that rely on simple keyword matching, these LLMs can pick up nuances. They can deal with synonyms, track references across multiple messages, and adapt to different writing styles. Since Copilot is embedded into Teams, it can apply its language understanding to your chat content, files, or meeting transcripts—based on the permissions you've granted. That means it's not just repeating memorized text; it's actually analyzing current, context-rich data to produce a relevant response.

Of course, the strength of an LLM depends on its training data. Microsoft invests heavily in improving these models while balancing performance, security, and privacy. Over time, Copilot's language abilities may get even sharper as the underlying LLM is updated or fine-tuned. Think of it as an ever-improving collaborator: the more it learns from user interactions (within the guardrails of data privacy), the better it becomes at anticipating your needs and clarifying complicated conversations.

Copilot doesn't operate in isolation. It's woven into the Microsoft 365 ecosystem, so it can "see" data from Teams chats, OneDrive files, Outlook calendars, or SharePoint libraries—only where permissions allow. When you request a summary of a channel discussion, Copilot taps into the chat transcripts stored in Teams. If you're scheduling a meeting, it might look at participants' calendars in Outlook to propose a convenient slot.

But don't worry—this doesn't mean Copilot free-roams your entire corporate data. The system respects user roles and organizational settings. If you're only allowed to access certain files in OneDrive, Copilot won't retrieve content from a folder you can't open. If a coworker's calendar is private or set to limited details, Copilot can't reveal any specifics about their schedule. This principle of "permission inheritance" ensures the AI's knowledge mirrors the same access constraints that apply to you as a user.

The key advantage is context. Because Copilot has that cross-service visibility, it can simplify multi-step tasks. For instance, if your team is chatting about a quarterly budget plan and someone references an Excel file in SharePoint, Copilot could locate and summarize that file if you have permissions. Or if you mention scheduling a follow-up, Copilot might propose an available timeslot after scanning relevant calendars, sparing you from flipping between multiple apps.

For Copilot to be truly helpful, it needs to process your messages and, at times, gather related files or schedule details. But how does the system ensure it only looks at what it's authorized to see? Typically, it relies on your existing Microsoft 365 identity. If you're a Sales Manager who has read access to certain customer records in SharePoint, Copilot can retrieve that content on your behalf—just as you would if you manually navigated there. Conversely, if you lack permission to view a certain project site, the AI can't rummage through it either.

This approach means Copilot acts much like a specialized user agent: it sits between you and the data, performing tasks you'd normally do yourself, but faster. If you're not granted access to a sensitive file, Copilot won't serve it up. Moreover, tenant-wide policies can restrict what kind of data Copilot can touch. For instance, an IT admin might decide that Copilot cannot process documents labeled "Highly Confidential," ensuring the AI can't accidentally surface restricted content in a summary.

Beyond simple file permissions, large organizations often set up role-based access controls (RBAC). For instance, finance staff might see budgets and invoices, while marketers cannot. Copilot respects these roles. The AI's domain knowledge about a piece of data is limited if you, as a user, don't have the clearance to access it. This means that if a finance conversation is locked down to certain individuals, Copilot cannot share or summarize that conversation with outsiders. This layered security posture ensures that AI-driven insights don't inadvertently leak information across departmental silos.

Furthermore, Copilot communicates with Microsoft's AI services using encrypted channels. Data is typically processed in memory, meaning it isn't permanently stored or visible to third parties. While details may vary as the service evolves, Microsoft's overall goal is to minimize the risk of data exposure while allowing beneficial insights. If your organization has compliance rules like GDPR or HIPAA, admins can configure Copilot's data-handling rules to align with these regulations, ensuring that everything from data residency to retention policies meets legal standards.

One question that arises with AI is: "Will it handle private or personal content responsibly?" Microsoft's approach to ethical AI includes guidelines for privacy, accountability, and fairness. For instance, if Copilot is summarizing a conversation that contains personal data, it won't broadcast those personal details to everyone. If it's asked to generate a summary of a channel that includes personal info, it attempts to omit or redact irrelevant private data. Of course, it can't do so perfectly all the time. That's why governance and user awareness remain crucial—if your team discusses highly sensitive topics in an open channel, consider limiting Copilot's involvement or using private channels that exclude the AI for those discussions.

Another aspect of ethical AI is ensuring transparency about how decisions or summaries are made. If Copilot highlights certain points in a chat summary, it's basically "choosing" which details matter most. Users might wonder: does the AI exhibit any biases in what it deems important? Microsoft invests in continuous improvement so the model avoids skewing highlights based on irrelevant factors. Nonetheless, biases can creep in from training data or incomplete context. The best practice is to treat AI suggestions as helpful leads, not absolute truths, verifying critical details as you would any other source.

User control is equally important. You might want to confirm a summary before sharing it widely, or to adjust an AI-generated list of tasks if you think Copilot missed something. Copilot tries to handle mundane tasks or help with preliminary drafts, but final decisions still rest with human judgment. If you find an AI summary inaccurate or incomplete, you can refine it or manually correct it. This collaboration between user oversight and automated assistance ensures responsible AI use, preventing the technology from making unchecked calls in high-stakes situations.

Sarah Reads an Internal Briefing on Copilot's Data Handling

Shortly after hearing about Copilot's pilot program at 365 Strategies, Sarah received an internal briefing from IT. The document explained that Copilot leverages large language models to interpret messages and glean context from Microsoft 365 data. It reiterated that AI respects existing permissions—so if Sarah lacked access to a certain project folder, Copilot wouldn't reveal anything about it. The briefing also reassured employees that the tool processes data in a secure environment and only serves up content they could already see themselves.

While reading, Sarah noted a section about user privacy and responsible AI. It mentioned that employees should label sensitive documents correctly, so Copilot wouldn't inadvertently summarize top-secret contract negotiations in a general channel. The briefing also described how the AI might produce drafts of emails or meeting recaps, but staff should check these for accuracy before sending them. "We're not letting the AI off the leash," joked the IT lead in the briefing; "It's more like a helpful coworker who still needs oversight."

Curious, Sarah hopped on a quick Teams call with someone from IT security to clarify a few points. She asked, "If I talk about a personal matter in a private channel, can Copilot see it?" The IT rep explained that if only Sarah and one other person have access to that private channel, Copilot can't share the content with a third party—it only surfaces content for authorized participants. However, they suggested avoiding personal details in unencrypted chat if possible, reminding her that while Teams is secure, it's still a work environment.

They also stressed the importance of using the correct metadata and classification labels on documents. "If you mark a file as 'Confidential—Legal Only,' the AI respects that," the IT person said. "We're setting up Copilot to skip those documents when someone else requests a summary." Sarah breathed a sigh of relief; she was happy to see the company balancing the convenience of AI with robust privacy measures.

Wrapping up, Sarah felt more confident about the tool. She realized that while Copilot's AI is powerful, it's carefully bounded by permissions and guided by best practices. "Okay," she thought, "this might actually lighten my load without opening any Pandora's box of data leaks." Eager to see it in action, she looked forward to the official rollout, envisioning fewer late-night searches for who promised to finalize a campaign design.

Understanding Copilot's AI underpinnings is key to trusting its help in Teams. By leveraging large language models that process natural language, and by integrating with your Microsoft 365 data responsibly, Copilot can offer suggestions and summaries that align with your real-time work context. Yet the system's capabilities only go as far as your permissions allow, preserving data security. Meanwhile, ethical considerations—like avoiding bias, maintaining transparency, and giving users final say—ensure that Copilot remains an aid rather than a risky free-for-all.

Sarah's experience highlights the importance of clarity around how an AI assistant handles your data. She found reassurance in her company's guidelines for data classification, user permissions, and the principle that Copilot is there to help, not override human judgment. In the next chapters, we'll move from this technical and ethical backdrop to the practicalities of setting up Copilot, training staff to use it effectively, and discovering specific ways it can automate tasks. As Copilot matures, you'll see how it becomes an increasingly indispensable coworker, turning daily chores into quick, contextual insights—while staying firmly within the boundaries you define.

CHAPTER 3: CONFIGURING COPILOT IN TEAMS

Getting started with an AI tool like Copilot may sound daunting, but the process is more about ticking the right boxes and understanding the basics of your Microsoft 365 environment than wrestling with complex technical details. This chapter will guide you through which licenses and settings are needed for Copilot, how to switch on its core features at the tenant level, and how you can customize AI options for compliance or security. Finally, we'll see how Sarah's IT department walks her through a straightforward enablement process—and how small configuration choices shape Copilot's overall effectiveness.

Before configuring Copilot, the first question is: Do you have the necessary license? Not every Microsoft 365 plan supports Copilot by default. Typically, you'll need one of the enterprise-level subscriptions that include advanced features—like Microsoft 365 E3 or E5—and possibly an additional add-on specifically for Copilot if it's not bundled into your plan. Microsoft occasionally adjusts its licensing bundles, so check official documentation or your company's licensing agreement. Your IT admin will likely confirm which tier you're on.

Sometimes, Microsoft also rolls out Copilot features in limited or preview form, letting certain customers access them ahead of a full public release. If you're part of a preview program, you might have extra steps—like signing up for a special pilot or agreeing to certain feedback terms. Whatever your situation, ensure you verify:

1. Which seats are eligible: If only certain employees have the premium license, Copilot might be limited to them, while others see no AI features.

2. Any add-ons: Some organizations must purchase a Copilot add-on for each seat.

3. Restrictions on region or data residency: In some geographical areas, Copilot might be delayed or subject to local compliance checks.

Beyond licensing, Copilot depends on a few system prerequisites. A common requirement is that your environment be relatively up-to-date—meaning you're running a supported version of Microsoft Teams, Exchange Online, SharePoint Online, and so forth. If your team still uses on-premises servers, talk to IT about hybrid setups. In some cases, partial integration is possible, but you might miss certain features if data remains offline.

You'll also need the right admin permissions to enable Copilot at the tenant level. Typically, a Global Admin or a high-level Teams Admin can switch on these services. They'll handle tasks like granting Copilot access to user data (within the parameters of your company's security policy). If your environment has granular admin roles, ensure the person configuring Copilot has the necessary scope.

At this stage, good communication between your business leads and IT staff is essential. Sometimes, employees assume Copilot automatically appears once they have a "Copilot license," but there might be additional toggles or disclaimers IT must set up. Knowing the licensing scope and system readiness upfront avoids confusion when you try to use AI features and they're nowhere to be found.

Let's assume your organization has the green light to deploy Copilot. The next step is turning it on at the tenant level—basically, the top-level switch that makes Copilot available across your Microsoft 365 environment. You can usually find these options in the Teams admin center or a related Microsoft 365 admin portal, depending on how Microsoft integrates Copilot in current releases.

The process might look like this:

1. Open the Admin Portal: Navigate to your Microsoft 365 admin center or the Teams admin center (the exact location can vary based on updates).

2. Locate Copilot Settings: Look for a section labeled "Copilot," "AI Settings," or something similar.

3. Enable or Configure: Flip the toggle or choose "Enable Copilot." Some admin centers present a brief wizard or advanced settings at this point.

4. Consent to AI Usage: Microsoft may request acknowledgment that you understand how Copilot processes data. Admins should review any disclaimers about data usage and privacy.

5. Save and Propagate: Once you hit "Save," it can take a short while—minutes or possibly hours—for the settings to propagate across the tenant, making Copilot's features available to end users.

After enabling Copilot, you'll see a set of default configuration options. For example:

- Chat Summaries: Do you want Copilot to offer summaries in every channel by default, or only in certain channels? An admin can decide how aggressive the AI's summarization suggestions are.

- Scheduling Suggestions: Copilot can propose meeting times by scanning participants' calendars. You can limit this to internal users, or let it factor in external guests (with certain constraints).

- Notification Preferences: Some organizations prefer a quiet approach, where Copilot only responds when explicitly asked. Others let Copilot proactively nudge users with "Did you mean to do X?" messages.

Think of these settings as the AI's personality dials. If your company is new to AI in the workplace, you might keep Copilot relatively quiet, letting employees get comfortable. Over time, you can open more advanced features as people see the value. Or, if your team is tech-savvy and eager, you could enable more proactive suggestions from day one.

Copilot's real value is in bridging data from multiple sources, but you might have external systems—like a CRM, a finance tool, or a marketing platform. If you want Copilot to incorporate info from those systems, you'll need to allow external data connections. This step might require setting up connectors or direct integrations, ensuring that credentials and APIs are in place. The admin center might prompt you to define which external services Copilot can query. If, for instance, your marketing data is stored in a separate database, you might need a custom connector for Copilot to read or summarize relevant info.

Keep an eye on security and compliance. If external data has sensitive details, confirm that only authorized users can see it. Copilot's advanced data retrieval should mirror your existing access controls—someone without clearance to an external system shouldn't see AI-summarized data from it. This typically means your external system or connector must handle tokens or roles consistent with your organization's identity framework.

Every organization has unique rules for data handling, especially those in regulated industries (healthcare, finance, government). If you handle personal health info or credit card details, you might want to disable or limit Copilot's ability to process those records. The admin portal may offer toggles like:

- Exclude certain SharePoint sites or label-based restrictions: If documents labeled "Highly Confidential" are off-limits to the AI, you'd configure that here.

- Disable certain AI actions: If you worry about AI drafting content in a compliance-heavy environment, you might turn off "Auto-Suggest Drafts" or require a user to confirm each suggestion.

- Audit Logging: For accountability, you might log when Copilot accesses or summarizes certain data, so your compliance team can review it if needed.

Balancing these security measures with user convenience is crucial. Being overly restrictive might hamper Copilot's usefulness, while being too lenient could risk exposing sensitive info. Most organizations refine these settings over time, starting with a moderate approach and adjusting as they see real-world usage patterns.

Walking Through Copilot Enablement with IT

At 365 Strategies, Sarah was on pins and needles waiting for Copilot. She knew it could summarize her busy marketing channel, potentially saving her hours of scanning. But first, IT had to officially "flip the switch." She scheduled a short call with Nina, an IT admin, to witness the enablement process firsthand.

During the call, Nina navigated to the Teams admin center and opened a new "Copilot Configuration" panel. Sarah watched as Nina confirmed their enterprise-level license included Copilot: "Yep, we're on E5 + the Copilot add-on for the pilot group," Nina said. She then enabled the feature at the tenant level, reading through a brief disclaimer about AI usage. "We have to confirm we've told employees about data handling," Nina noted, referencing the internal briefing Sarah had read. Sarah appreciated the transparency—IT wanted to ensure no one felt blindsided by new AI capabilities.

Next, Nina showed Sarah how to tweak a few default settings. By default, the system turned on chat summarization in all channels, but Nina proposed limiting that to the #Announcements, #Marketing, and #General channels initially, letting them test Copilot's summarization style. Nina then reviewed advanced settings—like scheduling suggestions. "We'll let Copilot propose meeting times, but only for internal participants for now," Nina decided, mentioning that external scheduling might come later. With a few clicks, Nina saved the configurations.

After hitting "Save," Nina explained that it might take a few hours for changes to propagate. She advised Sarah to keep an eye on the #Marketing channel to see if Copilot offered any summaries the next day. Sarah realized how even minor choices—like which channels to enable or whether to allow certain external data—would shape how much help Copilot provided. If IT had turned everything off by default, employees might barely notice Copilot. If they'd turned everything on, some might feel overwhelmed or worried about potential data exposure.

Sarah left the call feeling informed. She recognized that enabling Copilot was straightforward from a technical standpoint—mainly toggling options in the admin center—but the real art lay in balancing user adoption and data governance. "I like that we're testing it in just a few channels," she told Nina. "That way, we can see how folks respond and decide if we want to expand Copilot's reach later." Nina agreed, promising to loop back in a week for feedback. Sarah spent the rest of the day excitedly imagining how much time she'd save once Copilot started giving her quick recaps of marketing discussions.

Setting up Copilot might involve a few more steps than just flipping an "On" switch, but each step is crucial to ensuring a smooth rollout that respects your organization's structure and security needs. You'll need the right Microsoft 365 license, confirm your system meets basic requirements, and have the correct admin privileges to enable Copilot at the tenant level. From there, you decide how Copilot interacts with features like chat summaries and meeting suggestions, fine-tuning its scope to match your comfort level. If you're venturing into more advanced territory, you can open external data connections or apply strict compliance rules, depending on your industry's regulations.

Sarah's experience at 365 Strategies illustrates how small configuration details can shape whether employees find Copilot useful or intrusive. By enabling certain features gradually and focusing on channels likely to benefit, her company fosters a positive initial experience—encouraging staff to explore Copilot's potential. In the upcoming chapters, we'll dive into the real-time features Copilot offers—like automated chat summaries or action-item extraction—and how to harness them for maximum productivity. For now, rest assured that once you've handled licenses, toggles, and basic settings, you're on your way to letting AI lighten the daily load in Teams.

CHAPTER 4: INTELLIGENT CHAT SUMMARIES AND MEETING TRANSCRIPTS

One of the biggest challenges in a busy Microsoft Teams environment is keeping track of lengthy conversations and important decisions. Scrolling through a flood of messages or replaying an hour-long meeting can drain both time and energy—especially if you were out sick, on vacation, or simply focused on another project. Copilot's ability to summarize chat discussions and generate meeting transcripts offers a welcome solution. By automatically extracting key points, decisions, and action items, Copilot cuts through the noise. This chapter explores how Copilot handles chat summaries and meeting transcripts, showing you how to catch up on missed info without sifting through pages of logs. Finally, we'll follow Sarah as she returns to work after an absence and uses Copilot's features to get fully up to speed in record time.

The typical day in Teams often involves multiple channels, group chats, and direct messages. While it's great that everyone can share updates quickly, it's also easy to feel overwhelmed. Copilot alleviates some of that pressure by automatically generating summaries of chat threads. Whether it's a general channel with dozens of posts every day or a specialized project chat that had an intense debate, Copilot quietly reviews the conversation and, when prompted, produces a concise recap.

Under the hood, Copilot scans messages for recurring themes, mentions of tasks or deadlines, and back-and-forth decisions. It uses natural language processing to pick out phrases like "Let's do X," "We decided to revise the budget," or "Deadline is next Friday." From that, Copilot crafts a short overview that identifies main points, who said what, and any agreed-upon actions. It typically arrives as a brief paragraph or bullet list, so you can see at a glance what transpired. Some organizations configure Copilot to post these summaries periodically (like every evening) or only when specifically requested by a user.

A strong summary isn't just a random snippet of text—it highlights the *why* behind any conclusion, the *what* of each action item, and often, the *who* responsible. Copilot might write something like:

"In today's marketing chat, the team agreed to finalize the Q3 budget by Friday, with Maria revising the design mockups for the new campaign. Everyone decided to shift the product launch date from October 1 to October 15. Next steps include scheduling a follow-up meeting next Tuesday."

This level of detail ensures you don't just see that some discussion happened—you learn the specific tasks and any new timelines. If there's disagreement or unresolved points, Copilot often flags them, saying something like, "The group remains divided on which vendor to choose, with no final decision reached." That gives you a clue about the topics you might need to revisit or escalate.

Copilot also helps with meeting transcripts, a feature that has grown increasingly valuable as more teams operate remotely or across different time zones. During a Teams call, Copilot can generate a live transcript of who's speaking, capturing the conversation in near real time. This is separate from Microsoft's standard transcription—Copilot's intelligence can go further by summarizing segments or highlighting key decisions as the meeting unfolds.

Participants see the transcript in a side panel, or they can revisit it after the meeting. This is particularly handy if someone joins late; they can glance at the live transcript to see what was covered before they arrived. Or if you prefer a quick post-meeting recap, you can ask Copilot to summarize the transcript, creating a condensed version with bullet points around major decisions and tasks. This summary can be posted automatically in the meeting's associated channel or chat, so everyone has a single reference point.

After a meeting ends, the full transcript is typically saved to the meeting chat. Copilot can assist with editing that text—perhaps you want to remove off-topic chatter or fix minor errors in speech recognition. You might also highlight certain quotes or decisions. Then you can share the final transcript with relevant stakeholders, post it as a file in your project channel, or attach it to follow-up emails for external partners.

In more formal settings—like compliance reviews or project audits— these transcripts act as a documented record of who said what. That said, it's wise to confirm your organization's policies: some might require explicit consent to record or transcribe calls, especially if external guests are involved. If you're in a regulated industry, your admin might set up disclaimers or automatically disable certain Copilot features. Ultimately, the goal is to help employees reference past discussions easily, not to create more bureaucracy.

Let's say you were out sick, traveling, or pulled into a different project for a few days. Returning to a busy Teams environment can be daunting—unread messages, meeting invites, and random pings. Instead of manually scrolling through channels for hours, you can rely on Copilot to offer a quick summary of crucial chats. Ask something like, "Summarize the marketing channel from the past two days," and Copilot will produce a structured outline of key conversations, decisions, and next steps. If you need more detail, you can drill down further or check the original messages. But the summary speeds up orientation, letting you see if you missed any major deadlines or announcements.

Even if you're not out of the loop, you might face a scenario where a conversation spanned multiple days, threads, or side mentions. Maybe a finance topic popped up in the #ProjectAlpha channel, then moved to a separate #BudgetReview channel. Copilot's approach to summarizing saves you from rummaging in multiple places. You can request a summary of the relevant timeframe or ask Copilot specifically, "What were the final budget decisions in #ProjectAlpha for the past week?" The AI then surfaces the gist—like an instant cheat sheet.

Similarly, meeting transcripts come in handy after a particularly long brainstorming session or client call. Instead of re-watching an hour-long recording, you can scan Copilot's summary or read the transcript, searching for specific terms. For instance, if you recall the client mentioning "rollout plan," you can locate that exact mention in the transcript, see the context, and note the next steps without skipping through the entire video. This streamlined method ensures important details don't get lost or forgotten.

Sarah's Sick Leave and Quick Catch-Up

At 365 Strategies, Sarah woke up on Monday with a nasty flu. She emailed her manager, letting them know she'd be out for at least two days. By the time she returned on Thursday, her marketing channel had exploded with new posts about the upcoming product launch. Typically, Sarah would spend her first morning back reading hundreds of messages and possibly missing some key details. But now that Copilot was enabled, she simply typed into the #Marketing channel, "Copilot, summarize this channel's discussion from Monday to Wednesday."

Within seconds, Copilot produced a neat summary:

Project Launch Prep: Team decided on a new brand color palette; designers to provide final mockups by Friday. Lisa will finalize the revised budget. Next big milestone: stakeholder review meeting on Monday.
Vendor Updates: Two potential advertising agencies are shortlisted; final selection on Friday.
Open Questions: Deadline for shipping product samples still pending confirmation.

Sarah read that paragraph, then checked if there were any follow-up tasks for her specifically. Copilot noted, "Sarah to confirm the social media plan once the design is approved." Perfect—she knew exactly what to prioritize without scrolling through reams of chat.

On top of that, Sarah missed a major project update meeting on Tuesday, where the marketing and product teams aligned on the new timeline. Normally, she'd have to ask a colleague for highlights or watch the meeting recording. But after discovering the "Meeting Transcript" tab, she saw Copilot's live transcription had been turned on. The entire conversation was captured, and at the end was a Copilot-generated summary posted in the meeting chat.

Skimming the transcript, she found the moment the group discussed social media coordination. She noticed a mention: "We'll need Sarah to finalize the posting schedule after receiving the design assets," along with an agreed date of next Monday. That matched Copilot's summary in the channel. Sarah felt relieved that she hadn't missed anything crucial. Without devoting hours, she was fully caught up and could jump straight into her tasks.

In just 30 minutes, she was ready to proceed, feeling no confusion about what had transpired in her absence. Her manager was impressed: "I see you already found out about the new color palette and next milestone, good job!" Sarah grinned, thinking how just a few months ago, she'd have spent half a day playing detective in various channels and meeting notes. Thanks to Copilot's chat summaries and transcripts, she was back on track almost instantly.

Chat summaries and meeting transcripts offer some of the most tangible benefits of Copilot in Microsoft Teams. Rather than tediously scrolling through dozens (or hundreds) of messages, you can rely on AI to produce clear, concise overviews—pinpointing decisions, tasks, and who's responsible for what. The same goes for post-meeting reviews: searching for crucial details in a live transcript or simply reading a short summary can save hours, ensuring no important point slips through the cracks.

Sarah's experience underscores how these features can drastically reduce the chaos of missed communications, letting employees keep momentum on projects. Whether it's an unexpected sick day or just dealing with parallel projects, Copilot's intelligence spares you from manual catch-up drudgery. Of course, you'll still want to verify critical details or double-check an AI summary for completeness. But overall, these automation tools transform what used to be a chore into a quick, user-friendly experience.

In the next chapters, we'll explore Copilot's more advanced scheduling and task-generation features, plus how to handle data privacy, compliance, and best practices for maximizing its impact. For now, rest assured that with Copilot's chat summaries and transcripts, your team can focus less on rereading chat logs and more on innovating, decision-making, and moving projects forward.

CHAPTER 5: ADVANCED SCHEDULING AND TASK GENERATION

When you're juggling multiple projects, tight deadlines, and busy colleagues, two major headaches often arise: finding a time that works for everyone's schedule, and making sure no tasks or action items slip through the cracks. Copilot in Microsoft Teams aims to reduce these frustrations by scanning calendars to propose meeting times, sending out invites automatically, and even extracting action items from chats and meetings. This chapter explores how Copilot streamlines scheduling and task management, walking you through best practices so your team can coordinate effectively. Finally, we'll follow Sarah's story as she experiences fewer scheduling conflicts and sees how Copilot's "action item extraction" saves her from hours of manual follow-up.

Finding a mutually free timeslot can feel like herding cats—especially if your organization has multiple teams, varied time zones, or part-time employees. Copilot simplifies this by leveraging each participant's Outlook calendar data. When you request a meeting in a Teams chat or channel, Copilot looks at everyone's busy/free slots (limited by their privacy settings) and proposes options.

For example, if you type something like, "Copilot, schedule a 30-minute discussion with the Product and Marketing teams next week," the AI checks the relevant calendars for open windows. It then suggests a few plausible times that minimize conflicts. If you're part of a large group, Copilot can rank its suggestions, like "90% of participants are free on Tuesday at 2 PM, 75% free on Wednesday at 10 AM, etc." If external guests are included, Copilot might avoid times outside normal business hours or highlight potential time zone clashes, though these features depend on your organization's configuration.

Importantly, Copilot never overrides existing permissions. If someone's calendar is set to "Private," Copilot only sees that they're busy, not the appointment details. It can't magically reveal personal events or confidential meeting subjects. This keeps scheduling efficient but respects user privacy.

Once you choose a timeslot, Copilot can automatically send out the meeting invites. It typically drafts a short invitation message, which you can review or tweak before it finalizes. This might include a suggested title, like "Project Kickoff," and a brief agenda if you provided one. Everyone then receives an Outlook calendar event, plus a notification in Teams, ensuring they know about the upcoming session.

Copilot doesn't stop there. After scheduling, it can also set up follow-up reminders. For instance, you might want Copilot to ping participants a day before the meeting with a short recap of the agenda, or to remind them to review attached files. If your organization enables advanced features, Copilot might even gather RSVPs or prompt you to reschedule if too many people decline. Overall, the AI handles the tedious bits, giving you more space to focus on what the meeting is meant to accomplish rather than fiddling with calendar logistics.

Another big drain on productivity is pulling out actionable tasks from a sea of conversation. It's easy for crucial to-dos to vanish in a long chat thread or get overlooked once a meeting ends. Copilot addresses this by monitoring channels, chats, or transcripts for language that suggests a task—like "Could you handle X?" or "Let's do Y by Friday." Upon detecting these phrases, the AI can generate a list of potential action items.

For instance, if a Teams channel is discussing the next product launch, Copilot might compile tasks like:

- "Create new logo mockups" (Assigned to Lisa)

- "Draft social media posts by next Tuesday" (Assigned to Carlos)

- "Schedule user testing session" (Assigned to Alex)

The best part is that Copilot can take it a step further: if you have a tool like Microsoft Planner or To Do integrated, Copilot can automatically create tasks in the relevant Planner board, each assigned to the person it identified in the conversation. You, as the user, can confirm or adjust these suggestions—maybe reassign a task or change a deadline—before finalizing them. This saves an enormous amount of manual note-taking and ensures tasks don't slip through the cracks.

While Copilot does a decent job guessing who's responsible for which task (based on conversation context and mentions), it still occasionally asks for clarification if roles are ambiguous. For instance, if the chat says, "We need someone to finalize the budget," Copilot might not be sure whether to assign it to the finance lead or the project manager. In that case, it'll produce an "Unassigned Task" flagged for your review. If you manually set your preferences or mention "@FinanceLead, please handle this," the AI can capture that mention as the rightful assignee.

Once tasks are created in Planner or To Do, team members get notified, and the tasks appear in the standard Microsoft 365 task ecosystem. This unified approach means people can track to-dos from all corners of Teams—chats, channels, or meeting transcripts—without the confusion of multiple, scattered lists. Over time, Copilot's intelligence might recognize patterns, like if Lisa always handles creative tasks, it might preemptively assign similar duties to her (with your approval).

While Copilot's natural language processing can detect tasks fairly well, it's still beneficial to train your team to phrase tasks in a straightforward manner. For instance, typing "@Carlos, please finalize the FAQ doc by Thursday" is easier for Copilot to parse than a vague "We should probably get that FAQ doc done soon." Encouraging colleagues to mention names, deadlines, and clear verbs (like "finish," "draft," "review") helps the AI identify and assign tasks accurately.

Similarly, during meetings, if you adopt a quick verbal cue like "Action item: …" or "Next step: …," Copilot is more likely to spot it in the transcript. Over time, your team naturally picks up these habits, knowing that explicit language makes everyone's life easier. It also reduces the chance of tasks being lost if participants rely on memory alone.

When scheduling across multiple regions or time zones, Copilot's suggestions can help—yet it's wise to double-check for big time differences. You might tell Copilot, "Avoid scheduling meetings outside 9 AM to 5 PM in each participant's local time," so it looks for narrower overlapping windows. This approach may result in fewer available slots, but it respects everyone's work-life balance. If your projects involve external vendors or clients, you might also ensure Copilot recognizes their business hours if you have that data in your system.

As for tasks, if you need a deliverable from a team in a different time zone, Copilot can incorporate that difference into the schedule or deadlines. Still, human judgment remains vital if the AI picks an unrealistic due date. It's better to confirm with your remote colleagues than blindly trust an automated suggestion.

Fewer Scheduling Conflicts with Copilot's Suggestions

At 365 Strategies, Sarah's cross-departmental marketing group had a notorious history of scheduling conflicts. Two or three key people often found themselves double-booked or forced to skip important meetings. When Copilot became available, the team decided to lean on its scheduling suggestions for major project reviews. Instead of comparing calendars manually, Sarah typed "Copilot, schedule a 45-minute Project Launch review with the marketing and product teams next week."

Almost instantly, Copilot proposed three time slots that matched nearly everyone's availability. It also flagged that one product team member had an overlapping recurring meeting, advising either a half-hour shift or an exception. Sarah picked the best option, asked Copilot to send invites, and watched as a short summary popped up: "Project Launch Review— Attendees: Product Team (Alex, Jordan), Marketing Team (Sarah, Lisa, Carlos). Proposed Date: Tues 10:30-11:15 AM. Agenda: Finalizing brand assets, launching timeline." Everyone got the notification, and within minutes, all confirmed. The entire scheduling chore, which might have taken Sarah 20 minutes of emailing and Slack messages, was done in under two minutes.

Later that week, the brainstorming session for Q2 campaign ideas ran long. People threw out multiple suggestions: new ad formats, social media contests, potential influencers. The meeting ended with a broad agreement on tasks, but in the chaos, Sarah worried some to-dos might get lost. As the session concluded, Copilot posted a short summary in the meeting chat, listing the top five ideas and automatically extracting tasks like:

1. "Lisa to design mockup for influencer outreach strategy by Wednesday."
2. "Carlos to research ad platform metrics with a new partner."
3. "Sarah to create a draft schedule for the next 6 weeks of social media posts."

Sarah almost laughed at how seamless it felt: she hadn't typed anything to prompt this breakdown—Copilot had monitored the discussion, recognized key phrases, and assigned tasks based on each person's name. A quick glance reassured her that everything matched her mental notes. Without Copilot, she would have spent an extra hour writing a follow-up email or re-listening to the meeting recording to confirm who promised what.

By intelligently scanning calendars, parsing chats for tasks, and automatically generating updates, Copilot transforms two of the most time-consuming parts of collaboration: scheduling and action item tracking. Whether it's scanning Outlook availability to propose meeting slots or sifting through a heated debate to pinpoint the final decision, the AI spares you from tedious back-and-forth. Yet success hinges on good habits—labeling tasks clearly, respecting time zone complexities, and confirming any ambiguous assignments. As Sarah found, a few mindful tweaks (like using explicit mentions and deadlines) can elevate Copilot's utility and prevent missed responsibilities.

In the next chapters, we'll delve deeper into how Copilot can automate more routine tasks and even analyze conversation sentiment, plus the best ways to keep your data private and secure. For now, rest assured that advanced scheduling and automatic task generation can be some of Copilot's greatest gifts—cutting out busywork and ensuring your team remains tightly coordinated on every project. By adopting these features thoughtfully, you can finally break free from scheduling nightmares and vague follow-up action lists, letting your team focus on driving results.

CHAPTER 6: AUTOMATING ROUTINE TASKS AND ANALYZING CONVERSATIONS

By now, you've seen how Copilot can take a lot of the grunt work out of everyday collaboration—managing calendars, generating summaries, assigning tasks. But it doesn't stop there. Copilot can also help automate routine tasks that eat into your day and offer conversation sentiment analysis to gauge how your team (or customers) might be feeling. This chapter explores how Copilot fits into broader workflow automation, integrates with solutions like Power Automate, and lets you set up custom triggers for various scenarios. Finally, we'll follow Sarah again as she uses conversation analysis to detect negative feedback early, and sets up a few automations to keep her projects moving.

Many day-to-day tasks are straightforward yet time-consuming—sending routine status reports, copying data from spreadsheets into emails, or pinging coworkers for updates. Copilot aims to lighten this load by identifying these repetitive patterns in your Teams conversations or meetings. For instance, if a weekly chat about project milestones always ends with "Email the same update to the stakeholder," Copilot can learn that pattern and proactively handle it.

Imagine you have a shared Excel file where team members track sales leads. Each Friday, you usually email the results to management. With Copilot, you might say, "Copilot, please generate the weekly sales lead summary from the Excel document in #SalesChannel and email it to the management group." After a simple initial setup, the AI can gather the data, format a quick summary, and send it automatically, freeing you to focus on more pressing issues.

This approach blends Copilot's chat-based intelligence with workflow automation tools, taking routine tasks off your plate. Just remember that human oversight is crucial, especially at the start. You'll want to double-check the first few automated reports or messages to ensure Copilot captures the details accurately.

While Copilot can handle some automation within Teams on its own, it truly shines when connected to a bigger ecosystem like Power Automate. You might already be using Power Automate (formerly Microsoft Flow) to link different apps and services—like triggering an email whenever a SharePoint list gets a new item. Copilot can effectively act as a front-end for these flows, letting you initiate them with natural language requests.

For instance, if you say, "Copilot, create a task in Planner whenever someone posts 'urgent issue' in #CustomerSupport channel," Copilot might set up or suggest a relevant Power Automate flow. This synergy can drastically reduce the time it takes to build or modify workflows, because Copilot interprets your everyday language and configures the under-the-hood logic. As these tools evolve, you might see more advanced interplay where Copilot not only sets up the flow but monitors it for success or flags you if something goes amiss—like if a scheduled task fails to run.

One of Copilot's more advanced capabilities involves sentiment analysis—gauging whether a conversation's tone is positive, negative, or neutral. For internal teams, this might help managers track morale without relying on gut feeling alone. If Copilot detects a consistently negative tone in #Engineering chat, it might prompt someone to investigate issues or encourage a team-building effort.

Externally, if you have a customer support channel or a place where clients interact (possibly through a shared Teams channel or a connected platform), Copilot can parse messages for signs of frustration or dissatisfaction. Instead of waiting for a formal complaint, you might spot early grumblings, giving you a chance to intervene and address concerns before they escalate. The AI can even summarize major pain points, letting you quickly see if multiple customers are upset about the same product feature.

Sentiment analysis is only as good as the action you take afterward. If Copilot warns you that a group chat is trending negative, you can't just shrug it off. Maybe you ask Copilot to highlight the main criticisms or surface the relevant conversation threads. From there, set up a quick meeting or respond publicly to clarify misunderstandings or propose solutions.

A big advantage of AI-based analysis is spotting patterns humans might miss. If 80% of your remote workers' messages show signs of stress around deadlines, you might launch an initiative to streamline processes or reassign some tasks. If customers repeatedly mention a bug, you can escalate the fix. Over time, addressing these signals fosters a more responsive culture—people feel heard, and problems get tackled early.

While Copilot can autonomously notice tasks or schedule suggestions, you might want to explicitly define triggers for specialized workflows. For example, you can say, "Copilot, whenever someone types 'Overtime Request' in #HRsupport, create a new item in the OvertimeRequests Excel file and mention the HR lead." This ensures that key phrases instantly funnel tasks or data into the right place.

These triggers help you tailor automations to your unique business terms or abbreviations. Maybe you track project codes like "Alpha123" or have a nickname for an internal process. By telling Copilot to watch for those references, you ensure consistent follow-ups. But be careful not to overload your environment with too many triggers—too many automated posts can clutter channels if not carefully designed.

Automation is powerful, but it's not perfect. Copilot might occasionally misinterpret a sarcastic remark as a negative sentiment or create redundant tasks if the conversation is ambiguous. That's why most teams maintain a blend of AI-driven triggers and manual checks. You can let Copilot handle routine tasks but still require a human thumbs-up for sensitive actions—like sending an official client email or finalizing a large budget figure.

Think of Copilot as an assistant who drafts or prepares steps, but you, the human, do a quick review. Over time, if you see Copilot consistently getting it right, you might loosen the reins. Or if you notice a pattern of errors, reevaluate how your team phrases requests in chat or refine Copilot's triggers.

Sentiment Report for Customer Support Chats

At 365 Strategies, Sarah's marketing team occasionally deals with upset customers about promotions, product misunderstandings, or delayed shipping. They used to rely on anecdotal feedback—someone would say, "Wow, we've had a lot of complaints lately," but there was no systematic tracking. With Copilot, Sarah discovered a feature that could generate a sentiment report on the #CustomerSupport channel.

She asked Copilot, "Monitor #CustomerSupport for the next two weeks and summarize overall sentiment, noting any recurring themes." Copilot set up a watch, scanning messages daily. At the end of the period, it produced a short report: "Overall sentiment is 70% neutral or positive, 30% negative. Common negative themes include 'delivery delays' and 'incorrect item' references. Top repeated issue: confusion over return policy."

This gave Sarah and the support lead a clear direction—improve the clarity of shipping timelines and re-check the return instructions on the website. By addressing these specific pain points early, they managed to reduce future complaints. Sarah felt a tangible sense of relief—she didn't have to read every single message or guess at trends. The AI did the heavy lifting.

Sarah also experimented with automated follow-ups for her marketing projects. Typically, when a project hits a milestone—like finishing design mockups—she'd manually send an email to the stakeholder list, recapping progress and the next milestone. With Copilot, she simply typed in a dedicated "ProjectAlpha" channel: "Copilot, each time we complete a milestone in this channel, please draft a progress email to the stakeholder group."

She set up a custom trigger for "Milestone Complete" mentions. The first time someone typed "Milestone Complete: Design mockups done," Copilot generated a draft email summarizing the milestone, who worked on it, and what's next. Sarah checked it, tweaked a sentence or two, and clicked "Send." The result was a consistent communication flow for her stakeholders—no more forgetting to update them, and it only took a moment of her time.

From scheduling to-do reminders to analyzing overall conversation sentiment, Copilot can handle much of the daily digital drudgery that typically eats up time. By plugging into Teams' messaging and hooking up with external workflows like Power Automate, Copilot stands ready to transform how your team addresses routine tasks. The AI scans for triggers, identifies negative trends, and keeps an eye out for those critical next steps—all so your team remains aligned and proactive.

Sarah's story underscores how these features drive real value: an early warning system for customer dissatisfaction, automated progress emails that keep everyone in the loop, and a more streamlined approach to bridging chat and tasks. As with any powerful tool, balancing automation with human checks is wise—confirming that no message is taken out of context and that your workflow logic matches what your team actually needs.

In the coming chapters, we'll delve into data privacy, security, and compliance, ensuring that as you automate more tasks and analyze more conversations, you do so responsibly. But for now, consider how these advanced Copilot features can relieve your team from the grind of repeated manual steps, letting everyone focus on creative problem-solving and higher-level strategy.

CHAPTER 7: DATA PRIVACY, SECURITY, AND COMPLIANCE

As Copilot continues to handle more of your day-to-day tasks—scanning messages, summarizing chats, and linking data from various sources—it's crucial to remember that all this efficiency must coexist with data privacy, security, and regulatory compliance. Organizations handling sensitive or confidential information (or operating under strict regulations like GDPR or HIPAA) need assurance that the AI isn't violating user trust or exposing restricted content. This chapter explores how Copilot safeguards sensitive information, meets compliance standards, and maintains ethical AI practices. Finally, we'll follow Sarah as she discusses Copilot's data handling with her company's legal team, discovering why setting clear boundaries for AI usage is essential.

When you're typing in Teams, you might be sharing proprietary documents, discussing confidential deals, or referencing personal details. If Copilot has visibility into these messages (based on your permissions), how does it keep them secure? In most cases, Copilot relies on Microsoft 365's encryption protocols:

- At Rest: Data stored in Microsoft's servers (like chat history, transcripts) is encrypted. This means even if someone gains unauthorized access to the physical disks, the content remains scrambled.

- In Transit: When Copilot fetches a file from SharePoint or posts a summary in a Teams channel, that data is sent over secure channels (HTTPS/TLS). This encryption prevents eavesdropping on your network traffic.

Although Copilot processes content to generate summaries or suggestions, it isn't typically storing large amounts of data on its own—it uses existing Teams storage and memory. This approach ensures it can transform or analyze the data, but you're not duplicating records across random servers. Everything remains within Microsoft's data centers under your organization's tenant.

Some regulated environments (like healthcare) require special handling of personally identifiable information (PII) or protected health information (PHI). If you're discussing a patient's name or condition, you can't have the AI accidentally summarizing it for a user who lacks clearance. To address this, Copilot can redact certain data categories if they're flagged or if organizational labels are in place.

For example, you might configure a policy in Teams that any channel labeled "HIPAA Sensitive" triggers partial anonymization in Copilot's summaries. Instead of names, it might say "Patient #1234" or skip those details entirely. Additionally, some administrators choose to limit how long Copilot retains logs of certain sensitive channel analyses, automatically purging them after a set duration. These features protect both the organization and the end users from unauthorized data exposure.

General Data Protection Regulation (GDPR) in the EU requires that personal data be processed lawfully and that individuals have rights to access or erase their data. When Copilot handles user messages or personal info, it must abide by these rules. Microsoft provides documentation on how Copilot fits into the company's broader GDPR compliance strategy, typically ensuring that your data remains within specified regions if you have chosen data residency options. Your admin may configure the environment to store chat data in EU data centers, for instance.

HIPAA (Health Insurance Portability and Accountability Act) in the U.S. imposes strict rules on the handling of patient health information. If you're in healthcare, you might have already set up Teams with HIPAA-compliant channels, restricting who can join and how data is labeled. Copilot will inherit these compliance settings—if a channel is designated

HIPAA, Copilot respects that by limiting how it summarizes or shares content.

Other industries—finance, government, or defense—may have additional or specialized regulations, like FINRA or CJIS. In each case, the main principle is that if Microsoft Teams can be configured to comply with these laws, Copilot, as an extension of Teams, must follow the same guardrails.

To ensure accountability, organizations can audit Copilot's actions just as they track user activities in Microsoft 365. If Copilot generates a summary, it might log who prompted the summary and which data sources were accessed. This helps your compliance team verify that no unauthorized content was retrieved. If a user feels Copilot produced an unapproved snippet, the logs help identify if it was a misconfiguration or user error.

User consent can also be part of the workflow. In some setups, employees might see a prompt the first time they use Copilot, explaining how AI processes their data and providing an option to accept or decline. While not everyone may read the entire disclaimer, it promotes transparency and reduces the risk of employees feeling blindsided by AI processing private conversations.

While Copilot is advanced, it's not infallible. Like any AI model, it can mirror biases embedded in the data it was trained on or pick up incomplete context. For instance, if your team's conversation about job applicants includes ambiguous or biased language, Copilot might inadvertently highlight or summarize points in a skewed manner. To mitigate this, admins and team leads can:

- Encourage Inclusive Language: If your conversation is respectful and balanced, the AI's summaries are less likely to reinforce harmful stereotypes.

- Regularly Review Summaries: Spot-check Copilot's outputs for patterns that indicate bias—like consistently highlighting certain viewpoints while ignoring others.

- Use Balanced Data: If you're training advanced AI features (beyond the standard Copilot uses), ensure the training set or references are diverse.

Also, remember that Copilot's scope is limited by what data it can see. If your team is referencing incomplete documents or private sub-channel discussions, the AI might present a summary that omits critical details. Human judgment remains key to verifying that the AI's output is correct and well-rounded.

For ethical AI use, employees or external users should understand what Copilot is doing with their data. If Copilot is allowed to read a channel's messages, does it store them? Summarize them? Possibly mention them to other channels? Typically, the answer is that it only processes the data to generate insights for authorized viewers. But that must be communicated clearly. Some organizations post an "AI Usage Policy" pinned in relevant channels or share an FAQ explaining Copilot's capabilities and limitations.

Furthermore, if Copilot flags certain sentiment trends or automatically assigns tasks, it's valuable to show the reasoning: "Copilot assigned this task because the conversation said '@Lisa, can you finalize the brochure by Friday?'" This transparency prevents users from feeling the AI is making decisions behind the scenes without human input or accountability.

Sarah's Legal Team Review and Setting Boundaries

At 365 Strategies, Sarah began noticing how frequently Copilot summarized private channels and flagged potential tasks. While it mostly helped, she worried about the brand new "Product Roadmap" channel containing highly confidential plans. Could Copilot accidentally mention those details in a summary for a less restricted channel?

She reached out to the legal team for clarity. A week later, they scheduled a short meeting with IT and compliance. The discussion revealed that while the channel was private, Copilot recognized Sarah's right to see it—but if she asked for a summary in a public channel, the AI was configured not to pull details from private spaces. That setup was part of 365 Strategies' tenant-level policy. "We also have a label for top-secret channels," explained the compliance officer. "Those channels don't let Copilot operate at all. The AI can't see them." This relieved Sarah, who now understood the boundaries.

They also talked about how Copilot logs each summarized query in an audit trail. If legal needed to investigate a data leak claim, they could check if Copilot ever surfaced that info. The legal team recommended some additional disclaimers for employees, ensuring they knew Copilot's scope. Sarah left the meeting feeling reassured. She realized Copilot wasn't a free-roaming AI scraping all corners of the network. It followed the same roles and security design as any user.

Still, Sarah decided to set up a few channel-based rules. For instance, the marketing channel rarely needed to see finance details, so she added a label there, limiting Copilot's summarization to that marketing content only. "It's better to draw clearer lines," she thought. "That way, no one fears an accidental mention of a finance doc." Through this process, Sarah came to appreciate the nuanced trade-off: you get efficiency gains from AI, but you must define guardrails to keep data safe and meet compliance needs.

Data privacy, security, and compliance are cornerstones of Copilot's deployment. While the AI can handle tasks and generate summaries, everything hinges on robust encryption, inherited permissions, and the right governance policies—especially in regulated industries. Meanwhile, ethical AI considerations require vigilance against bias, a respect for user transparency, and fail-safes that prevent unauthorized data exposure.

Sarah's story highlights how a bit of planning—using private labels, limiting certain channels, and auditing the AI's actions—can alleviate fears about uncontrolled data flow. As your organization integrates Copilot deeper into its workflows, balancing convenience with compliance ensures that the benefits of AI-driven summaries, task extraction, and conversation analysis do not overshadow the critical need to protect sensitive information. Next, we'll explore best practices for maximizing Copilot's impact in your day-to-day routines and how to cultivate a culture that embraces AI responsibly.

CHAPTER 8: BEST PRACTICES FOR MAXIMIZING COPILOT'S IMPACT

By this stage, you know what Copilot can do—summarize conversations, schedule meetings, assign tasks, and even analyze sentiment. Yet leveraging these capabilities to the fullest requires more than just flipping a switch. You need to teach people how to interact effectively with AI, manage user adoption so skepticism doesn't stall progress, and set up feedback loops that keep Copilot improving. This chapter delves into best practices for phrasing questions, building trust around AI usage, and fostering a mindset of continuous improvement. In the end, we'll see how Sarah hosts a "Copilot tips and tricks" session at 365 Strategies, helping her colleagues grow more comfortable and productive with the AI's features.

If you've ever tried to ask a search engine something vague—like "What's happening with my stuff?"—and gotten irrelevant results, you understand the importance of clear, concise queries. Copilot, although more context-aware than a generic engine, still benefits from specific prompts. Instead of "Summarize last week's chat," you might say "Copilot, please summarize the key decisions from #ProjectAlpha between Monday and Friday." This extra detail helps the AI produce a more focused overview.

Encouraging your team to use direct action verbs also helps. "Copilot, create a task for Carlos to finalize the design by next Wednesday" is easier for the AI to parse than "Maybe we should have Carlos do something about design?" The more precise the wording, the better Copilot can identify what's needed. Short training sessions or internal docs on "How to talk to Copilot" can guide employees to:

- Mention relevant channels, time ranges, or file names.

- Use direct references to deadlines, outcomes, or tasks.

- Provide context like "for the marketing team" or "for the project review" so Copilot knows the scope.

Copilot can't be the solution for every query, especially if your question is extremely broad or out of Copilot's domain (like deeply technical references outside your company's data). If you simply want to find a document name you recall partially, a direct Teams or SharePoint search might be faster. Similarly, a well-organized knowledge base can sometimes beat AI if you know the exact location of an FAQ or policy manual.

A good rule of thumb:

- Use Copilot if you need a summary, an action item extraction, or something that spans multiple data points across chats and documents.

- Use direct search if you have a precise query like "Find file named 'BudgetQ4.xlsx.'"

- Use your knowledge base if you're dealing with established, structured information like a step-by-step process that rarely changes.

Over time, your team develops an intuition about which approach yields the fastest, most accurate results. Copilot excels in bridging context—like combining chat insights with scheduling—but a straightforward search might still be best for a single piece of known data.

Introducing AI into any workplace often stirs up questions: "Will it invade my privacy?" "Is it accurate?" "Am I going to lose my job to a robot?" These concerns deserve open discussion. One way to ease fears is by showing quick wins—small but meaningful use cases where Copilot saves time or effort. For instance:

- Display how it can schedule a tricky multi-time-zone meeting in seconds.

- Demonstrate how it summarizes a chaotic 200-message channel into a clear, actionable list of items.

When employees see that Copilot reduces mundane tasks without replacing the unique human touch—like creativity, empathy, or problem-solving—they become more receptive. This approach also helps them trust Copilot with bigger tasks down the line. A short internal showcase or a lunch-and-learn session can highlight these successes. Let volunteers share their positive experiences, like "I used Copilot to recap yesterday's client call, and it caught things I almost forgot!"

It's natural for some team members to worry about automation encroaching on their roles. The reality is that while Copilot can automate certain routine tasks—like drafting follow-up emails, summarizing transcripts, or proposing meeting times—it's not built to replace human creativity, decision-making, or interpersonal skills. Emphasize that the AI is a tool to enhance productivity, not a substitute for human employees.

Leaders can reinforce this message by reassigning time freed up by Copilot to higher-value activities. If employees used to spend hours manually transcribing meetings, they can now focus on brainstorming new ideas or refining customer experience. By framing AI adoption as augmenting rather than replacing human roles, you nurture a culture of innovation and reduce anxiety.

Even the best AI can produce off-target suggestions occasionally—maybe it misreads a sarcastic remark in chat or assigns tasks incorrectly. The key is having a feedback mechanism. Encourage users to flag inaccurate summaries or mention when Copilot misconstrues context. This might involve a short rating system (like thumbs up/down on AI suggestions) or a dedicated channel where people can report odd Copilot behaviors.

Admins or AI champions can review these reports regularly, identifying common threads. Perhaps the AI struggles with certain jargon or abbreviations in your industry. Or maybe it consistently misses tasks if they're phrased in a roundabout manner. By analyzing feedback, you can refine Copilot's triggers, adjust AI settings, or train your team to phrase tasks more explicitly. This iterative loop helps Copilot become more aligned with your organization's style and needs.

Once you see benefits—like Copilot summarizing a marketing channel or assigning tasks for weekly stand-ups—you'll likely spot other workflows ripe for AI assistance. Maybe your legal department needs Copilot to track contract approvals, or finance wants help with daily budget checks. As you pilot new scenarios, gather metrics: how many hours saved, how many tasks caught that might have been forgotten?

Periodically revisit workflows to see if you can push automation further or if certain steps need more human checks. You might discover that some tasks require partial AI involvement—like drafting a summary— while other tasks remain purely manual. Aim for a balance: enough automation to lighten the load, but not so much that employees feel overshadowed or confused by too many AI interventions.

Hosting a "Copilot Tips and Tricks" Session

At 365 Strategies, Sarah noticed that while some colleagues loved Copilot, others barely used it—or typed vague commands that led to subpar summaries. She decided to run a short "Copilot Tips and Tricks" session during lunch, inviting anyone curious. She showed real examples: how to ask for an "Action-Item Recap from yesterday's #Marketing chat," or "Copilot, schedule a 30-minute budget review next week with the finance team." She explained the difference between using Copilot and direct search, plus reminded them to keep sensitive data in private channels labeled accordingly.

Enthusiasm grew as people realized how easy it was to prompt Copilot for something like "Show me unresolved tasks in the design thread since Monday." A coworker from product support piped up, "I had no idea it could scan an entire chat for tasks. That'll save me hours!" Another asked how to handle accidental tasks Copilot might assign. Sarah reassured them that they could either unassign the task or correct Copilot, so it adapts over time.

Post-session, Sarah noticed an uptick in Copilot usage. More channels had pinned messages with best practices: "Use direct language like '@Copilot, create a task' or '@Copilot, show me this week's marketing updates.'" People also grew bolder in trying out advanced scheduling or action extraction. With these quick wins, the "Copilot fear factor" faded. Even longtime skeptics realized it wasn't replacing them; it was liberating them from mundane chores.

The feedback loop also improved. Users reported any weird summaries—like missing context or misread jokes—in a dedicated #CopilotFeedback channel. IT periodically checked these logs, tweaking configurations. Over a few weeks, Copilot's suggestions became more spot-on. Colleagues praised Sarah for the session, saying, "We didn't realize how much we were underusing Copilot until now."

Maximizing Copilot's impact requires more than technical enablement—it demands a mindset shift in how teams approach everyday collaboration. By teaching employees to phrase prompts precisely, showing them clear benefits, and establishing a feedback process, you transform Copilot from a curious add-on into a trusted assistant. And by addressing concerns around AI's role, you reassure staff that their human expertise remains central, while repetitive tasks are offloaded.

Sarah's experience proves that a few well-planned demos or training sessions can spark a wave of confident usage, drastically raising Copilot's value. As we move into the final chapters, we'll look at how to troubleshoot and validate AI outputs, plus peek at the future of Copilot in Teams—ensuring your organization stays on the cutting edge without sacrificing clarity or control. For now, consider hosting your own "tips and tricks" session, gather user suggestions, and watch as your team discovers new ways Copilot can enrich their daily routines.

CHAPTER 9: TROUBLESHOOTING AND VALIDATING AI OUTPUTS

Even though Copilot can handle many daily tasks—summarizing chats, extracting action items, scheduling meetings—it's not infallible. Like any AI tool, it occasionally produces odd suggestions, overlooks key points, or misinterprets jargon. This chapter focuses on troubleshooting common Copilot issues, validating AI-generated content, and escalating problems when necessary. Finally, we'll see how Sarah at 365 Strategies deals with Copilot occasionally misunderstanding niche industry terms, prompting her to report feedback and apply a temporary workaround.

Inaccurate Summaries: Sometimes Copilot's summaries might omit a crucial decision or mix up who said what. This could happen if the conversation was ambiguous or if certain relevant messages were in a private channel where Copilot lacked permissions.

Missed Tasks: You might expect Copilot to assign a follow-up task after a meeting, only to find it never appeared. Often this occurs if the conversation lacked clear trigger words, like "Action item," or if the chat ended abruptly with no mention of who should handle the task.

Irrelevant Suggestions: Occasionally, Copilot proposes tasks or meeting times that don't align with your actual context. Perhaps it misread a joke as a serious to-do or recommended a timeslot that overlaps with a major company event. These errors typically reflect incomplete context or a misinterpretation of user intent.

Each of these issues can be frustrating, especially if your team relies heavily on Copilot to keep them organized. The good news is that diagnosing them often pinpoints a straightforward fix—like refining your usage patterns, adjusting the AI's access settings, or feeding it more precise prompts.

When Copilot produces unexpected results, consider these root causes:

1. Permissions Misalignment: If Copilot doesn't see all relevant channels or files, it can't generate comprehensive summaries. Check if the channel in question is private or labeled "Confidential," restricting AI analysis.

2. Data Fragmentation: Maybe your conversation spanned multiple channels, or you keep referencing a file in a separate location. If Copilot sees only part of the puzzle, its output may be incomplete. Consolidate data where possible, or specify a channel/time range in your prompt.

3. Incomplete AI Training: Although Copilot arrives with robust language capabilities, it can still struggle with specialized jargon or brand-new concepts. If your team uses unique acronyms or slang, Copilot might misinterpret them. Over time, feedback and usage help the AI adapt, but occasional hiccups are normal.

When investigating issues, start by confirming that Copilot has the correct permissions to the channel, user, or SharePoint folder. Next, see if the conversation was scattered or filled with ambiguous phrasing. If none of these stand out, you can typically log a feedback ticket with Microsoft or check community forums to see if others face a similar glitch.

For all Copilot's convenience, you shouldn't blindly trust every AI-generated snippet or to-do. A best practice is to quickly review each summary or list of tasks, especially for high-stakes projects or external-facing communication. Here are some validation tips:

1. Cross-Reference: If Copilot says, "The team agreed on a new launch date of October 1," skim the actual chat thread for a moment to confirm.

2. Ask Follow-Up Questions: If you're unsure about a missing detail, say, "Copilot, did anyone discuss the budget changes in that chat?" You might uncover additional context or confirm the budget was never mentioned.

3. Compare With Meeting Notes: If you took manual notes or had a designated human note-taker, cross-check them against Copilot's output. Substantial discrepancies might signal an AI misunderstanding.

Beyond everyday usage, you can also gather user feedback through short polls: after big summaries, ask the channel if it was accurate or if any major points were missed. This real-time polling fosters collaborative improvement.

AI can accelerate decision-making but shouldn't replace human judgment. If Copilot drafts an email or sets tasks with certain deadlines, a quick user glance can confirm the details are correct. This step is crucial for external emails—nobody wants to send a misunderstanding to a client. Over time, your team grows comfortable with Copilot's accuracy on routine items, while maintaining vigilance on sensitive or complex decisions.

Emphasize that employees hold final responsibility for verifying content. Reinforce that "AI is a helper, not a manager." This mindset ensures you don't end up in tricky situations where Copilot's misunderstanding leads to wasted effort, conflicts, or compliance issues.

When Copilot acts unpredictably, or you face a unique scenario, it's time to tap into broader support:

- Microsoft Resources: Check official documentation or troubleshooting guides. Microsoft often updates Copilot's known issues or tips for advanced configuration.

- Community Forums: Online communities where other admins and users share experiences can be invaluable. You might find that your niche issue (like AI misreading certain jargon) has a workaround.

- Internal AI Specialists: Larger enterprises may have an AI or data science team. If so, they can help refine your usage patterns or build custom solutions that feed Copilot more context or handle specialized tasks.

The key is not to feel isolated. AI is still evolving, and user feedback often drives Microsoft to refine Copilot's capabilities. If you find a genuine bug—like Copilot repeatedly ignoring a channel's settings—report it through your organization's official support channel or directly to Microsoft's feedback link, if available.

Copilot thrives when it receives feedback loops. If you notice repeated misinterpretations of certain terms, don't just shrug—tell Microsoft or your AI champion internally. Suggest a new feature or propose a refined approach: "We keep referencing 'alpha build' in #DevChannel, and Copilot always thinks we're talking about a new product name. Could it differentiate between alpha builds and alpha product lines?"

Such requests often feed into Copilot's future updates, which might roll out fixes or expansions. If a bug severely impacts your workflows, a direct escalation ensures your voice is heard. Over time, these reported issues shape how Copilot evolves for all users.

Misinterpretation of Niche Jargon at 365 Strategies

At 365 Strategies, Sarah's marketing group began noticing oddities: Copilot assigned tasks that made no sense. It seemed to interpret their custom acronym "RAS" (short for "Request a Sample") as a general English word, occasionally marking it as negative sentiment or pulling it into irrelevant to-do lists. For instance, whenever someone typed "We need RAS from the design team," Copilot would post a summary about a "raspy tone in the discussion" or "action needed to fix the 'ras' task."

Sarah realized that the acronym confusion was messing with Copilot's usual efficiency. She first confirmed that Copilot had the correct permissions and none of the channel settings were blocking it. That was all fine. So it seemed the culprit was simply a vocabulary gap.

Sarah contacted their in-house IT lead, who recommended logging feedback via a "Copilot Feedback" channel in Teams. She attached examples of the misinterpretation. IT escalated it to Microsoft's feedback portal, explaining how RAS was a unique abbreviation at 365 Strategies.

In the meantime, they instituted a short workaround: instruct employees to type "ReqSample" instead of "RAS" or to mention "RAS (Request a Sample)." This additional context clues Copilot in, reducing confusion.

Though not an instant fix, Sarah noticed Copilot's misunderstandings dropped significantly. By clarifying the abbreviation or using the spelled-out form, the AI recognized it as an action item. Over the next few weeks, a few employees tested if "RAS" was still misread, seeing small improvements. Eventually, a Copilot update might arrive that better handles user-submitted glossaries or specialized acronyms—thanks in part to Sarah's feedback.

Troubleshooting and validating AI outputs are integral steps in fully embracing Copilot's capabilities without letting mistakes derail your workflow. Whether you face inaccurate summaries or strange task assignments, investigating issues usually reveals solvable causes—like permission overlaps, scattered data, or misunderstood jargon. Meanwhile, validating Copilot's suggestions helps maintain trust, ensuring employees still apply human judgment for critical decisions.

Sarah's story of misread acronyms illustrates how user feedback loops and minor adjustments can resolve 80% of misinterpretations, while official bug reports drive longer-term fixes. As your team grows more reliant on Copilot's automation, these feedback and troubleshooting processes become second nature. In the final chapter, we'll glimpse the future of Copilot in Teams—how AI-driven features might expand even further, shaping a workplace where repetitive tasks fade, and creativity thrives. For now, remember that an AI assistant works best when users feel empowered to correct, refine, and guide it—turning initial hiccups into incremental improvements.

CHAPTER 10: THE FUTURE OF COPILOT IN TEAMS

Through the previous chapters, we've explored how Copilot can reduce busywork, keep projects organized, and enhance conversation analysis. But Microsoft's AI journey is far from finished. New updates and features are always on the horizon, promising deeper integrations, improved intelligence, and even voice-based assistance. This concluding chapter looks ahead to Copilot's future in Teams, discussing upcoming capabilities, the broader business impacts of AI-driven collaboration, and how you can position your organization to remain at the cutting edge. We'll close with a final glimpse of Sarah's evolving plans for 365 Strategies, as she anticipates new voice features and next-gen tools.

One of the most anticipated developments for Copilot is multilingual support. While it already handles many languages at a fundamental level, Microsoft aims to refine real-time translation and localized summarization. Imagine Copilot bridging language gaps in multinational teams—instantly summarizing Spanish or French chat threads into English, for example. As globalization intensifies, these improvements can unify scattered offices or streamline cross-border projects.

Deeper analytics are also on the roadmap. Currently, Copilot summarizes chats and meeting transcripts, but future expansions could include advanced topic clustering, project-related sentiment analysis, or trend detection over extended periods. For instance, if your #CustomerFeedback channel sees a surge in negative sentiment around a product feature, Copilot might highlight that pattern in a monthly insight report, letting you respond proactively.

Meanwhile, voice-based AI interactions could significantly shift how we communicate with Copilot. Instead of typing prompts or reading text summaries, you might verbally ask, "Copilot, what decisions did we make about the new app design last Friday?" The AI would reply with a voice-based summary. This hands-free approach could be especially helpful for people working on the go or in roles where typing is inconvenient—think warehouse supervisors or traveling sales reps.

Copilot is already integrated with Teams and, by extension, Outlook calendars, SharePoint documents, and more. Yet Microsoft aims to push these integrations further, unlocking synergy across the entire Microsoft 365 ecosystem. For example, imagine Copilot pulling advanced data from Microsoft Project to identify risk factors in a schedule, or referencing advanced analytics from Power BI to enrich your meeting's summary with real-time metrics.

Beyond Microsoft's own suite, expect deeper partnerships with third-party platforms. If you rely on Salesforce, Slack channels integrated with Teams, or specialized software like ServiceNow, you could see new connectors that let Copilot unify these data sources. The AI might provide a single command center, bridging multiple tools so you don't have to switch context continuously. This evolution mirrors the industry's push for "one-stop-shop" experiences, where collaboration, data, and intelligence converge in a single workspace.

As Copilot and similar AI assistants mature, many predict a fundamental shift in collaboration. Right now, we actively ask Copilot to summarize or schedule. Down the line, the AI might proactively nudge us—"I see you're discussing budget overages. Would you like me to pull last month's financial breakdown?" or "You've mentioned launching a new campaign. Should I fetch the brand guidelines?" This context-aware approach can minimize friction, letting teams move fluidly from idea to action.

Workflow changes could be profound. Employees may rely on AI suggestions for triaging emails, generating first drafts of reports, or scanning through complex documentation. Daily stand-up meetings might revolve around automated progress recaps, letting participants focus on problem-solving rather than re-stating to-dos. Departments like finance, HR, or marketing could find synergy as Copilot helps them coordinate tasks that once required endless email chains. The lines between roles might blur, as individuals lean on AI for tasks outside their traditional expertise—like a marketing specialist quickly drafting legal disclaimers with Copilot's help (and, of course, final review from legal).

Right now, we've often viewed Copilot's impact on a team or project level. But imagine entire departments harnessing AI. Finance could use it for generating monthly close reports or analyzing cost anomalies. HR might let Copilot handle routine onboarding queries or summarize employee feedback from various channels, allowing HR staff to focus on complex personnel issues. Marketing could rely on Copilot for real-time competitor analysis (if integrated with external data) or drafting campaign proposals.

When multiple departments share this AI-literate culture, cross-department synergy flourishes. For example, if Sales sees a surge in certain customer questions, they can rely on Copilot to relay that info to Product and Marketing, prompting swift adjustments or clarifications. Essentially, by bridging data silos and speeding up knowledge transfer, Copilot fosters a more agile, responsive organization.

If you're eager to explore Copilot beyond this book, a great starting point is to define clear goals and metrics. Instead of vaguely hoping AI will "improve collaboration," pick tangible measures:

- Time saved: Track how long it used to take for tasks like meeting scheduling or chat scanning, then measure after Copilot adoption.

- Task completion rate: Note if more tasks get captured and completed on time.

- User satisfaction: Send out short polls every month. Are people finding summaries accurate, or do they regularly need to correct them?

- Reduction in manual overhead: If employees used to spend X hours per week on repetitive tasks, see how that number changes.

Gathering these metrics helps demonstrate ROI to leadership and identifies areas needing improvement. Maybe Copilot's scheduling suggestions are spot-on, but chat summaries remain patchy. These insights guide further training or configuration tweaks.

Microsoft frequently updates Copilot's features. Some updates might require admin toggles, new licensing add-ons, or user training to appreciate newly introduced commands. Keep an eye on Microsoft 365 Roadmap pages, official Teams blogs, or community forums. If your organization is large, you might designate an internal "Copilot champion" who stays informed and shares relevant updates. This approach ensures you don't miss out on new functionalities—like advanced analytics or voice-based AI—that could reshape how your teams collaborate.

Regularly checking these channels also signals your organization's readiness to join pilot programs for early features. Sarah's company at 365 Strategies, for example, hopped on Copilot's pilot, gleaning immediate benefits and shaping the AI's design through feedback. If you stay engaged, you too might influence Copilot's direction, ensuring it aligns with real workplace challenges.

Looking Forward to Voice-Assisted Copilot

At 365 Strategies, Sarah has witnessed how Copilot's chat-based features transform daily routines. She recently caught wind of a rumored voice-assisted Copilot update in Microsoft's next big release. According to insider notes, employees could soon talk directly to Copilot—asking it to schedule a meeting or summarize a chat just by speaking a command in a Teams call. For people working remotely on the go, that could be a game-changer.

Intrigued, she loops in her department's leads and the IT admin. "We should prepare a pilot group once the voice features drop," she suggests. The marketing lead loves the idea of quickly telling Copilot, "Check the Q2 campaign channel for unresolved tasks," while in the middle of a brainstorming session. However, the IT admin advises caution: "We'll need to confirm language support, plus ensure the voice recognition respects user privacy. Let's gather user feedback upfront to see if there's real demand."

Anticipating these new possibilities, Sarah drafts a short plan. She proposes continuing the "Copilot tips and tricks" sessions each quarter, highlighting fresh updates. She also suggests refining the organizational guidelines so that employees who prefer voice commands get comfortable using them, while those who'd rather type can still do so. She envisions a near future where employees seamlessly chat with Copilot verbally, obtaining immediate data or generating quick tasks, further cutting manual overhead.

As she finalizes her presentation for upper management, Sarah feels a sense of excitement and responsibility. Copilot's evolution has already revolutionized how her teams share information and handle tasks. Taking the lead in adopting next-gen AI features not only boosts efficiency but positions 365 Strategies as an innovative workplace where employees feel empowered by technology rather than hampered by it.

The future of Copilot in Teams is bright and fast-evolving. As Microsoft rolls out multilingual support, deeper analytics, and possible voice-based interactions, AI stands to reshape workplace communication on a broader scale. This shift promises cross-department synergy, letting finance, HR, marketing, and more seamlessly exchange insights and respond quickly to changing conditions.

For you, the reader, the next steps involve setting goals, tracking metrics, and staying tuned to Microsoft's roadmap. By regularly updating your Copilot configuration, training your workforce, and exploring new features, you ensure the AI remains a helpful, dynamic collaborator.

Sarah's forward-thinking approach at 365 Strategies offers a glimpse of what's possible: a workspace where routine tasks are handled automatically, crucial decisions get ample real-time data, and employees spend their energy on creativity and innovation.

As you close this book, remember that Copilot's true potential lies in how well it complements human expertise, not how it replaces it. With thoughtful deployment, transparent policies, and ongoing feedback, your organization can continue to leverage AI-driven collaboration features that elevate productivity and keep you at the cutting edge of digital transformation.

EMPOWERING COLLABORATION THROUGH COPILOT AND BEYOND

By now, you've seen how Copilot can transform daily collaboration in Microsoft Teams—from generating quick chat summaries and automating tasks, to offering scheduling suggestions and even analyzing sentiment. You've explored the core technology behind it, delved into important security considerations, and learned best practices for adopting AI at work. Through Sarah's stories, we've witnessed both the excitement and the practical steps needed to make Copilot a reliable digital ally in your organization.

At its heart, Copilot is about reclaiming time and energy. By handling repetitive chores—like sifting through endless chat logs or figuring out everyone's availability for a meeting—this AI tool frees you to focus on creativity, problem-solving, and meaningful human connections. Even though Copilot offers impressive features, it thrives best in an environment where users are encouraged to provide feedback, refine workflows, and trust the AI while verifying critical outputs.

Reflecting on Key Takeaways

1. Understanding AI in Teams

    o Copilot works alongside your existing Microsoft 365 data, respecting user permissions and organization-level security. Whether you're summarizing a project channel or scheduling a cross-department meeting, Copilot taps into the same data you can already access, only faster and more context-aware.

2. Configuring for Success

    o Proper licensing, tenant-level settings, and a few best practices around channel labels and user prompts can make Copilot more accurate. Remember, you can toggle features on and off to match your organization's comfort level, gradually exposing more advanced capabilities as people adapt.

3. Boosting Day-to-Day Efficiency

   o From summarizing multi-day threads to extracting tasks from meeting transcripts, Copilot spares you from busywork. When connected with workflows like Power Automate, it can automate entire sequences—sending updates, flagging deadlines, or scanning for negative sentiment in customer chats.

4. Maintaining Security and Compliance

   o AI only helps if it doesn't jeopardize sensitive data. Setting up the right guardrails—through encryption, data retention policies, and role-based permissions—ensures you're getting the benefits of AI without risking privacy breaches or regulatory missteps.

5. User Adoption and Continuous Improvement

   o People are often curious but cautious about AI. Demonstrating quick wins, addressing fears of job replacement, and encouraging feedback are key to sustained Copilot use. As the AI gains trust, employees can offload more mundane tasks, devoting time to strategic work.

6. Staying Prepared for the Future

   o Microsoft's roadmap hints at advanced language features, voice-based commands, deeper analytics, and broader integration with external apps. By keeping an eye on these updates, you'll ensure your team remains competitive and continues to evolve with the technology.

If you found this exploration of Copilot helpful, there's more to discover. The Microsoft Teams Companion Series covers every facet of Teams, from fundamental setup to specialized use cases:

- Introduction to Microsoft Teams: Perfect for newcomers learning about basic licensing, user roles, and best practices for rolling out Teams across a company.

- Teams & Channels: Focuses on organizing people and projects, exploring channel moderation, channel structures, and how to scale Teams in large organizations.

- Chats & Meetings: Dives into everything from direct messages to large-scale webinars, breakout rooms, and best practices for remote or hybrid meeting success.

- Teams Phones: Guides you through integrating telephony with Teams, covering calling plans, advanced features like auto attendants, and how to replace legacy PBX systems.

- Apps & Integrations: Shows you how to extend Teams beyond simple collaboration, integrating third-party apps, custom connectors, and the Power Platform for custom solutions.

- Accessibility in Microsoft Teams: Explains how to create inclusive workspaces, with features like Immersive Reader, live captions, and meeting tools designed for all users.

- Microsoft Teams in Education: Tailors Teams for classrooms and academic institutions, complete with assignment workflows and parent-teacher communication tools.

- Security, Compliance, and Administration: Delves deeper into advanced governance, data loss prevention, retention policies, and large-scale admin best practices.

- Expert Tips & Troubleshooting: Offers power-user hacks, script examples, and solutions for common issues, ensuring you can keep Teams running smoothly.

Each book in the series uses real-life scenarios—often starring Sarah or other everyday professionals—so you can see how theoretical best practices translate into on-the-ground improvements.

Implementing Copilot or any AI tool is a journey. If your team starts with small steps—like letting Copilot summarize a single high-traffic channel or schedule a few routine meetings—they'll soon see how much time it saves. As trust builds, you can roll out more advanced features, train your staff to craft precise AI prompts, and integrate the AI deeper into critical workflows.

If challenges arise—be it a missed task or an inaccurate summary—approach them as learning opportunities. Encourage users to provide feedback, refine prompts, and possibly adjust your AI settings if the environment is highly regulated. Over time, the synergy between human expertise and AI support leads to a more efficient, forward-thinking culture.

And remember: AI doesn't replace human roles, it augments them. By offloading manual overhead, employees gain space to tackle strategic, creative, and relationship-based tasks that AI can't replicate. This opens new horizons for professional growth, letting people develop higher-level skills instead of slogging through repetitive chores.

As you move forward, keep the lines of communication open—whether through short training sessions, feedback channels, or internal champions who track new Copilot updates. Your organization's success with AI hinges on collaboration, transparency, and a willingness to adapt. If you treat Copilot as a dynamic partner—one that evolves with your business and receives continual feedback—you'll find that each incremental improvement further cements an AI-enhanced culture of efficiency and innovation.

Ultimately, Copilot's most profound impact lies in freeing your team to think bigger. Rather than rummaging through logs or coordinating schedules, employees can devote energy to problem-solving, creative brainstorming, or forging deeper client relationships. As Microsoft refines the AI and adds new capabilities—like voice interactions or specialized analytics—your organization can keep pace by staying informed and open to experimentation.

We hope this book has equipped you with the insights, best practices, and confidence to integrate Copilot effectively into Microsoft Teams. While the path involves learning curves and occasional bumps, the payoff is a more agile, cohesive, and forward-looking workplace. And if you're hungry for more ways to optimize your Teams experience, the rest of the Microsoft Teams Companion Series awaits—each volume opening a new door to advanced features, specialized scenarios, and real success stories.

Here's to a future where AI-driven assistance becomes second nature, collaboration flows seamlessly, and your team's collective intelligence shines through every conversation and decision. May Copilot be a steadfast partner on your journey toward continuous growth and success in the modern digital landscape.